C000217311

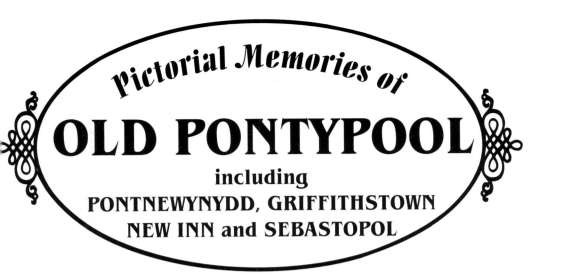

Pictorial Memories of OLD PONTYPOOL

including
**PONTNEWYNYDD, GRIFFITHSTOWN
NEW INN and SEBASTOPOL**

by Bryan Roden

Foreword by
The Rt. Hon Paul Murphy, MP
Secretary of State for Wales

Volume 2

Old Bakehouse Publications

Abertillery

First published in October 2000

ISBN 1 874538 04 2

Published in the U.K. by
Old Bakehouse Publications
Church Street,
Abertillery, Gwent NP13 1EA
Telephone: 01495 212600 Fax: 01495 216222
http:/www.mediamaster.co.uk/oldbakebooks

Made and printed in the UK
by J.R. Davies (Printers) Ltd.

Foreword
by The Rt. Hon Paul Murphy, MP
Secretary of State for Wales

I have enormous pleasure in writing this foreword to the second volume of Bryan Roden's *'Pictorial Memories of Old Pontypool'*. Bryan's first book was deservedly, an outstanding success. Indeed, it was given to me as a special 50th birthday gift by my Secretary, Irene!

Bryan is a true native of our valley. Like me, he went to West Mon. School, and again like me, he has a deep feeling for Torfaen's past. By publishing such fascinating photographs, Bryan has provided future generations with a remarkable record of life in Pontypool over many years. Without his efforts, it is quite possible that these remarkable records would have been lost forever.

I am sure that the many people - from all over the world - who read this excellent book will find great pleasure in matching their personal memories to the photographs. In addition, historians of the County Borough will find great treasures in its pages.

I congratulate Bryan on this outstanding publication, and as Member of Parliament for Torfaen, thank him for illustrating our rich historical heritage so vividly.

Contents

Introduction

It is some two years since Volume One in this series of Pontypool books was first published and, as to be expected, the inevitable question arose - *'When is Volume Two due to appear?'*. The demand for my first book was grossly underestimated, resulting in two reprints and consequently, I hope that this latest volume will be just as well received and live up to everyone's expectations. During the interim period between these two books, in co-authorship with Malcolm Thomas, *'Pictorial Memories of Old Abersychan'* was published and this met with similar success. The circulation of both books has been very intriguing and widespread, with numerous copies reaching the Americas and Australasia which suggests that Abersychan's and Pontypool's ancestors have travelled afar over the years.

Two years seems a very short period of time between the publishing of two Pontypool books, and yet, significant changes have still taken place and will probably continue to do so. The town centre for instance, is a victim of unabated decline with two well-known businesses locking their doors for the last time. Larcombes, the sports shop has since closed and the long-established and reputable furnishers of C.H. Pearce is no more, a shop that traded in the centre of Commercial Street for more than eighty years. This is the pattern of events that has now driven so many shoppers to such places as Cwmbran and further afield to make their purchases. I'm sure that there are many readers who will remember the days when Pontypool had shops galore but nowhere to park, now it is a town with plenty of parking space but with an on-going deficiency in shopping facilities.

Local industry has also suffered, the principal cause of urban decay, and such famous names as British Nylon Spinners, Pilkingtons and H.G. Stone are now consigned to the history books. The final chapter in the book is devoted to the *'then and now'* situation, and should be of particular interest to younger readers who, out of necessity will ask, *'Where was this and where was that?'*.

This latest publication is not intended to be depressive or invite suggestions that we might be 'living in the past', it merely aims to record an important and agreeable heritage and accept progress for what it is. Having said that, the vital question still remains - *'What does the future hold?'*. The answer to this probably rests in the hands of the economists, who need to be persuaded to bring back the jobs and investments to our town, the future will then look after itself.

To everyone who has bought and read Volumes One and Two in this Pontypool series and the Abersychan production, I extend my sincere thanks for your continued support and encouragement.

Special thanks are also due to The Rt. Hon. Paul Murphy, MP Secretary of State for Wales who kindly provided the forewords for both the Abersychan book and this latest volume of Pontypool.

Bryan Roden

CHAPTER 1

Pontypool Town and its Vicinity

1. The pictorial tour of Pontypool begins with Crane Street in the year 1906 and towards the upper part of the street is the old railway bridge, originating from around 1850 and one of a number of the town's former landmarks removed during the last decade. Nearest to the camera and on the left, an elderly gentleman with his faithful companion appears to be stepping into the White Lion public house; the premises are nowadays occupied by optometrists W. Phillips and Son.

2. A busy scene in Crane Street from about 1917, on this occasion looking down from just above the Three Cranes Hotel. On the opposite side of the street is the three-storey building belonging to Mr. Daniel Wheatley Simpson. Founded in the late 1890s, Mr. Simpson's business was advertised as tailor, clothier, hatter and hosier - he also being a well-respected member of the local council and deacon at Mount Pleasant Congregational church.

3. The narrowness of old George Street, seen here from Commercial Street during the 1930s, was forever a subject of heated debate amongst the community. Reports from the year 1910 for instance, tell of unceasing complaints from locals to the council concerning horses, carts and carriages continually throwing up dirt and mud everywhere. Even after the demise of horse-drawn transport, motor vehicles were frequently seen mounting the pavements, much to the distress and safety of pedestrians.

4. Moving back in time to the Edwardian era, the picture illustrates early George Street. At number three, the ornate lamps belong to clockmaker and jeweller Albert Allmark whilst further along the same side of the street are the shop signs of Masters, Cash & Co. and Olivers, all familiar names from the past. On the opposite side and nearest, is the premises of stationers and booksellers Edwards & Co. with boot and shoe dealer W. Charles next door.

5. This photograph, looking towards The Cross, was probably one of the last taken of old George Street before demolition of this side of the thoroughfare was undertaken in July 1963. Business premises such as Dean's, Moss's, The Maypole and Full Moon Hotel all disappeared for good with no replacements being opened in the town.

6. An almost deserted Commercial Street in 1905. On display is the well-known ornamental lion belonging to Fowler's store, a reminder of the former White Lion Inn (licensed premises not to be confused with its namesake in nearby Crane Street).

The White Lion was built on the site of another much older inn, The Blue Boar which was demolished in about 1840. Immediately opposite is a building with inscribed tablets on its façade, this being the earlier structure of the old corn market, built in 1730 by Mrs. Frances Bray, daughter of Sir Edward Morgan of Llantarnam and Lady of the Manor of Wentsland and Bryngwyn.

Besides housing the town's first market, the upper floor of the building was the principal venue for public meetings and theatrical performances, attracting numerous well-known Thespians of the period. It was also the most commodious room in Pontypool until the present Town Hall was opened in 1856.

The occupants of the building at the time of this photograph were Messrs. Hughes & Son, printers and stationers who continued to trade here well into the 1980s. On the extreme left of the picture, under the occupancy of Mrs. James Williams and part of which is just visible, is the Cross Boot-Warehouse. A few years later this was knocked down to make way for the London City and Midland Bank. In earlier times it was the site of the Red Lion Inn, Pontypool's leading hotel and stopping point for stage-coaches, the rear of the building incorporating a coach-house and stables.

The room already mentioned above the corn market was also once used as a club room for the inn, and whilst there is uncertainty as to the origins of this ancient structure, records do exist of a meeting being held there as early as May 15th 1778.

7. Almost one hundred years have passed since this impressive view of Crane Street at the junction with Market Street was taken. On the corner, Jones's have an exterior display of their wares and the young lads appear to be assisting in the removal of some goods. This store, which was later renamed Manchester House, was originally founded by a Mr. Evan Jones who was described as a draper and silk merchant. In later years the shop was purchased by Mr. A.C. Fowler and became known more familiarly as *'Top Fowlers'*. These days the site is occupied by a pharmacy store with the local *'Job Club'* on the floor above.

8. This original picture postcard from about 1910 is captioned *'From the quarry Pontypool'*, and was photographed from just below Broadway, showing an area that has changed quite beyond recognition during the past few decades. In the centre of the picture a goods train passes through Crane Street Station, today the site of the town's bypass and to the left of the footbridge, is the station's goods shed and yard. Nearer to the eye on either side of the railway line, are the buildings which formed part of the top end of Crane Street itself, with Montague Terrace on the right, all now gone.

9. Another part of the town that has seen a few alterations since being photographed here in 1908, is Market Street. The Wheatsheaf Inn, Davies the butcher and the Market Tavern together with the white-fronted buildings further down have long been demolished. The market building itself was erected on the Blue Boar Field which also had another, not too inviting name, *'The Bloody Field'*, it being an unofficial venue for infamous brawls. Less alarming forms of entertainment were also most popular here such as travelling shows, miniature theatres, boxing booths and funfairs.

10. A damp-looking Commercial Street in late Edwardian times with, on the right, an elderly couple passing the grocery shop of James Knapp at number 31, which is now the location of Torfaen Gallery. Next door is the once-popular stationers W.H. Smith who in later years moved to larger premises further along the street nearer the library. Two doors away at number 25 is another name from the past, that of Eastman's butchery shop.

11. The years have now moved on in Commercial Street to the 1960s with two businesses of note in view. Nearest are stationers W.H. Smith whose earlier shop is mentioned in the previous photograph. Next door is the central store of the Abersychan and Pontypool Co-operative Society which was opened on March 31st 1938 by General Manager Mr. H.D. Cotton. At the time, this emporium which took more than two years to complete at a cost of over £32,000, compared favourably with the largest stores to be found in many cities. Unfortunately at present the building stands empty, facing an uncertain future.

12. A typical scene in Hanbury Road during the 1950s when, as today, the up-valley bus stop was situated outside the Town Hall but with down-valley buses stopping in front of the park gates. Bus transport in the 1950s was well-patronised and with competition from the valley's train service to last but a few more years, well-known bus companies such as Western Welsh, Red and White, Ralph's and local firm Peake's enjoyed a prosperous period.

13. The imposing Carnegie Library as seen on a picture postcard from 1908, the sender of the card commenting *'at last Pontypool can boast of a free library'*. The whitewashed wall to the left remained intact for more than twenty years before part of it was removed for the building of new premises for W.H. Smith's and the Co-operative Society, as seen on the previous page and adjoining the Commercial Street shops at the far end.

14. A well-adorned Hanbury Road during the Royal Welsh National Eisteddfod Week of August 1924. Attracting large crowds from far and wide, the Eisteddfod's foremost event was the visit by the Prince of Wales. To welcome the prince on his arrival, many thousands of people lined the route from Pontypool Road Station to the park where he was greeted with a civic address read by chairman of the council, Mr. D.C.Udell.

15. Another look at Hanbury Road from the opposite direction during the 1960s, long before the need for the 'traffic-calming' system in place these days. The road, which had lost its extended stone-built wall some years previous to make way for the bus stops, has two motor vehicles of the day including a mini van, making their way out of town past the former 'fifties style' shelters.

16. An early panoramic view overlooking the town with the upper part of Crane Street in the foreground. On the extreme left, the street's Tabernacle Baptist Church is visible and in the background are the well-cultivated park gardens. To the upper right of the picture and before any housing development at Penygarn, are the distant buildings belonging to Penygarn Farm.

17. A quiet day in Osborne Road is captured during the 1930s with a number of latter day businesses to be recalled. These former traders include Masters (clothier), Major & Son (ladies and gents tailor), Melias (grocers) and Wildings (clothiers and outfitters). Further up the road just past the parked cars, is yet another familiar name from yesteryear, Roath Furnishers.

18. Proceeding approximately one hundred metres beyond the Roath Furnishers and the scene at Osborne Road is a far cry from today's roadway with its abundance of traffic. The shop seen here on the near right (now converted into flats), is advertising something from the past - Welsh flannel shirts at factory prices. Adjacent to the shop are the premises of the National Telephone Company and around the time of this photograph, the business was in the capable hands of Mrs. Matilda Smith. Just a few doors further on, the shop with the extended canopy at Number 90 is that belonging to Mr. William Adams.

19. A wide-ranging view from about 1906 featuring Clarence Corner to the right and the once common sight of a coal train heading down the valley. To the right of the train's rear engine are the premises of one of Pontypool's many respected traders Stanley M. Williams, advertised as an iron and hardware merchant and brewer. In the foreground are the stationary coal wagons belonging to John Blindell's Black Vein Steam-Coal Collieries of Pontypool whilst to the left, are some three and four-storey buildings situated in Limekiln Road.

20. A much closer look at Clarence Corner with the imposing Clarence Hotel and Carlton Cafe in sight. This scene pre-dates the construction of the new Free Press offices which were completed and opened to the right of the café in 1923, an event taking place after more than thirty-two years of printing at Osborne Road. The business remained as such until 1985 when it was again transferred to new premises at Pontymoile Corner.

21. Some additions and alterations have taken place in this similar view of Clarence Corner, the period having moved on to the late 1960s. A much larger roundabout has been built to contend with increased volumes of traffic and the former Pontymoile Corner lamp, now minus its ornate top (as seen on page 35) has replaced its predecessor. Other additions are the offices of both the Red and White Bus Company and the Free Press on the extreme right.

22. This view overlooks the town of Pontypool from Penygarn Hill in the year 1905 and most noticeable is the fact that the houses now on Broadway (top right) have not yet been constructed. The prominent white-fronted building in the right foreground stood at the bottom corner of Lower Crane Street, a street once known as Japan Street. This particular building is believed to be where the manufacture of the famed Pontypool Japanware was once produced.

23. The date of this photograph taken from the bottom of Penygarn Hill is April 1976, not too long ago and yet the changes by today's standards are quite significant. The area is seen being cleared to make way for the new roadway which would by-pass part of the town from Commercial Street, via Riverside, to the upper part of Osborne Road thereby relieving the then traffic problem through the town centre. Business premises removed at the time of the upheaval included monumental mason Ken Jones and a garage owned by the General Post Office.

24.   A distant view of The Folly in the year 1900, with the ancient buildings in the foreground belonging to Nant-y-Gollen Farm, Trevethin situated adjacent to Folly Lane, at the time occupied by farmer William Evans. The farm, believed to date from the sixteenth century, still forms part of the Pontypool Park Estate and at present is one of the few farms still working in the area, producing organic beef from a herd of Aberdeen Angus cattle. The current tenant is Mr. Steve Warman who resides close-by at the converted 'Old Barn' Pant-y-Gollen, his father Glyn occupying the Nant-y-Gollen farm house.

25. As already mentioned, the tenant at the time of the above photograph was Mr. William Evans whose family occupied Nant-y-Gollen for about sixty years until 1956. Pictured left is Mr. Evans with some of his family and they are, left to right - Back: younger daughter Annie, an unidentified neighbour and younger son Ivor. Seated: William Evans, his wife Martha and daughter Augusta. At the front is a young orphan boy named Trevor.

26. A substantial procession is seen under way at Trevethin in the year 1900 and is obviously of some importance as it includes military personnel, a brass band and at the forefront, members of the local fire brigade in classic brass headgear. The view of Leigh Road includes in the background, the ancient building of Trevethin Church. To the left of the church is 'Wern Farm' and an age-old barn once used as a Sunday School.

27. Penygarn housing estate as seen from The Grotto sometime during the 1950s. The estate, built in the mid to late 1920s, was constructed as part of the local council's housing redevelopment programme to replace numerous slum dwellings then in the locality. November 1936 presented a momentous occasion for the residents of Penygarn when His Majesty King Edward VIII paid a brief visit to the estate as part of his tour of the south Wales valleys. The king was said to be quite distressed upon hearing that one in three of those living in Penygarn at the time was unemployed.

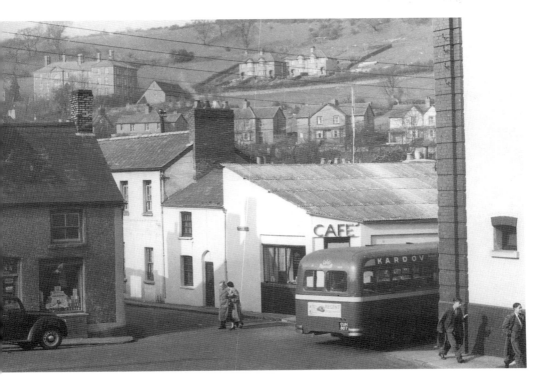

28. Another memorable picture from the 1950s, this time at Pontnewynydd and nowadays this scene would be difficult to recognise, every building in the foreground having been demolished. It is the junction of Hill Street (left), George Street (centre) and Mill Road to the right and is sure to revive a few memories for many readers of this book. A Western Welsh bus is seen passing between the Pavilion Cinema and Pelopida's Café, on its way to the garage at the rear of the cinema.

29./30. Two distinctive views of St. Luke's Road Pontnewynydd. The picture above, from about 1908 is taken from the entrance to the galvanising works and shows the former drinking fountain (minus its lamp) which was erected and unveiled in 1899. This impressive structure was the conception of local colliery-owner and J.P. Mr. Edward Jones who resided at Snatchwood House, later to become Snatchwood Hospital. At the opening ceremony the fountain was presented to the Abersychan Urban District Council, having been made available thanks to the generous subscriptions by residents of the Pontnewynydd ward. The view below, a more distant look at St.Luke's Road in 1911, is seen from just below Hospital Road with the rear of the nearest housing belonging to George Street.

31. This scene, almost a reversal of the previous photograph, is a view of Pontypool Hospital from St. Luke's Road during the same period. The buildings in the centre are also situated in, or near to George Street and the structure partially hidden by the tree is one of Pontnewynydd's long-standing hostelries - the Royal Oak; this public house is still trading today when many others in the area have closed down or been completely demolished.

25

32. A panoramic study from 1914 looks up the valley towards Abersychan. The industrial buildings in the foreground form part of Pontnewynydd's sheet and galvanising works and just above, right of centre, is seen the Primitive Methodist Chapel on Hanbury Road. This chapel, once part of the Park Terrace circuit, was later to amalgamate with the Wesleyan Methodist, eventually changing its name to the Methodist Church. Closure came in 1970 after almost ninety years of worship, followed by the inevitable demolition and the construction of new housing on the site.

33. Pontnewynydd, looking in a southern direction is pictured from a spot just below Club Row Snatchwood in 1910. The scene overlooks Freeholdland Road in the centre and Snatchwood Board School situated in Lower Leigh Road (top left). This school, a fine example of late Victorian architecture, has served the children of the community for almost one hundred years since its opening in 1901.

34. This is an alternative distant look at Snatchwood School during the late 1930s. In the extreme right foreground are the buildings and stack belonging to the Eastern Valley Co-operative Steam Laundry, and nearby is the site where the former Monmouthshire canal terminated. The canal, constructed in the 1790s by engineer Thomas Dadford junior, opened to traffic in 1796 and extended from Newport to Pontnewynydd wharf where local industries were connected by tramways, enabling transportation of their minerals.

35. A 1940s observation of Pentrepiod as viewed from Pen Rhiw Franc with in the distance, the once-familiar stacks of Pontnewynydd works. Left of centre the buildings once belonging to Pentrepiod Farm may be seen and, just visible to the left, in front of the tree are *'White Houses'*. Right of centre, by the middle tree are *'Greenland Cottages'*, since demolished and replaced by a more modern structure.

36. Plas-y-coed Road, in amongst its industrial surroundings as it appeared just before the outbreak of World War One in 1914. Left of centre and just above the houses is Gwenallt Colliery (The Jack Pit) and in the distance above the Gwenallt is the ill-fated Llanerch. It was here in 1890 that an underground explosion claimed the lives of 176 men and boys in what was the worst mining disaster ever to hit the eastern valley of Monmouthshire. To the right of the houses, more former industrial landmarks are featured such as Cwmnantddu's Oak Brick Works with the track above leading to the steam-emitting Viaduct Colliery.

37. Moving on to Wainfelin and this early scene depicts a rather sombre occasion - a funeral in Rosser Street. About to lead the cortege are members of the Salvation Army Band who are standing in front of Peake's horsedrawn hearse, with the family mourners at the rear. Looking closely in the background, it can be seen that house number 60 in Wainfelin Avenue, is still in the hands of the builders.

38. The year is 1914 in Wainfelin Avenue and it will be noted that the road surface is in need of some improvement. On the left is Irvine Morgan's shop and stood outside are two young local ladies; they have been identified as Keturah (Kate) Mary Jones who is facing the camera and stood in front, looking down the Avenue, is her elder sister Hetty Adwin Jones.

39. The Tranch, with a lone collier making his way up the hill and this is yet another area of Pontypool that has changed so much since this photograph of some 85 years ago. The cottages on the extreme left are still standing but have since been converted into a single dwelling, which is now number 28. One other building to survive is the house furthest away on the right with its tall chimney prominent above the bush.

40. This early view of Albion Road in 1908, is looking towards the old railway bridge situated near Clarence Corner. The bridge, now demolished, was originally constructed when the Monmouthshire Railway Company built their line between Newport and Pontypool some sixty years previous. Also disappeared, are the typical Victorian-designed houses on the right which were built for local workers in the nineteenth century. Just beyond the houses is the Albion Inn which is now the site of a petrol filling station.

41. A 'Bird's Eye View' from the early 1950s looking towards the Cwm Glyn Valley with Pontypool Park in the foreground and if studied carefully, it will be seen that many more changes to the environment have taken place since. Left of centre is the railway line heading towards Hafodyrynys, the western valleys of Monmouthshire and beyond. There are a number of reminders of an industrial past such as the former waste tips in the background, whilst in the bottom left is the gas works sited near Mill Road Trosnant with the chimney stack belonging to the old Limekiln aside the railway track.

42. In its heyday Pontymoile Junction was the 'gauging stop' for the canal's commercial traffic, determining the toll which would be payable at the junction's cottage. This was done by measuring the 'freeboard', that is, the distance from the water to the upper edge of the boat. The procedure was, that a measurement would be taken in two places on either side of the vessel, with an average calculated to ascertain the precise charges due on the cargo and payable to the resident toll clerk. Besides being an office for the toll keeper, the cottage was also the home of the 'ganger' or 'lengthman' whose responsibility it was, to keep a particular length of the waterway in good working order.

43. A scene of tranquillity in Lodge Woods Pontymoile, long before the construction of any housing which began in the 1960s. Today, in the year 2000, the scene has altered somewhat, the landscape having been decimated, with Pontypool Park Estate receiving a measurable amount of local criticism for felling the majority of the woodland thus destroying the afforded privacy and pleasant environment.

44. The ancient houses of Trosnant in 1903, a district of Pontypool that developed with an influx of workers who came from many parts of Great Britain seeking employment in the local forges and works during the Hanbury era. Whilst not entirely proved, it is believed that Trosnant was the location where the first specimens of the world-renowned and much sought-after Pontypool Japanware were manufactured.

45. A part of Trosnant that many readers will probably recognise even today. Pictured in the early years of the twentieth century, the scene shows one of the town's early ash carts doing its duty collecting from the rear of the Hanbury Hotel. The building in the centre, which is now a garage, was at one time the local registry office, the premises dating from the year 1837. On the extreme left, just past the gas standard and with Clarence Street in the background, is the protruding sign belonging to another of the district's hostelries, the Waterloo Inn, then standing at number one Trosnant Street.

46. An unusual view which was photographed from a window of the Clarence Hotel by one of its guests in August 1938. The house in Clarence Street to the left foreground was known as Trosnant Lodge and at the time, was occupied by two of the town's eminent medical practitioners - Mr. Bertram Siddons M.B. and Mrs. Enid Siddons M.B. Directly above the Lodge is a closer look at the premises of Stanley M. Williams who is mentioned in picture number 19, his property now appearing to be vacant. On the far right are some more old buildings sited below Lower Bridge Street.

47. Dating from the 1960s or early 1970s this aerial view overlooks Lower Bridge Street. The detached bay-windowed house which is left of centre and positioned at the entrance to the caravan park was, in earlier times, owned by Mr. Cornelius Rich a local tradesman. Mr. Rich was a confectioner whose sweet factory was the long building situated on the opposite corner to his house, both of which are now sadly demolished. As well as the factory, Mr. Rich managed a shop in Crane Street and a stall in Pontypool Market Hall.

48. This setting at Pontymoile Corner dating from the 1930s, should be compared to an earlier, but similar view on page 23 in Volume One of this series of Pontypool books. It will be seen that the demolition workers were also in business 70 years ago, with a number of buildings on the left now gone. Further down the road, the Pontypool Motor Company's Park Garage has appeared and, on the decorative lamp is a warning sign '*Dead Slow*', an essential necessity for the gradual increase in motor traffic that plagued this part of Pontypool for so long.

49. These fine houses in the lower part of Victoria Road were erected towards the end of the nineteenth century, during the reign of Queen Victoria, from whom the road's name was probably adopted. The house which stands alone in the background and now known as *'Southleigh'*, was originally built and occupied by Mr. Thomas Morgan Wintle who named it *'Bethany'*; Mr. Wintle and his wife were joint founders of Pontymoile Mission Hall.

50. Rockhill Road, looking south towards Pontymoile Corner in the year 1913 features a crowded procession, an event that took place quite often during the early years of the last century. This, a military parade heading towards the town, appears to contain a mixture of old soldiers and young recruits. The houses seen in the background are known as Waverley Terrace with the year 1904 inscribed in the stonework, thus confirming the year of their original construction.

51. This is how part of Cwmynyscoy appeared during the 1930s and as usual many changes have taken place since. In the background are the houses situated at Blaendare Road and prominently in the foreground is a public house which is still there today, the Wheatsheaf Inn. A long-lasting popular 'local', the pub still retains its exterior appearance and has outlived the adjoining abodes on either side, more modern housing having appeared during the last few decades.

52. These former ancient dwellings originally known as *'Firtree Cottages'* were situated on Prescoch Lane which leads from the now-abandoned Prince of Wales public house (The Tump), to Penyrheol. The cottage on the right named *'The Firs'*, was demolished almost twenty years ago and its neighbour *'Fir Tree'*, after standing derelict for a number of years, has been transformed using the original stone. This new structure is now unrecognisable when compared to the above late-nineteenth century picture.

53. This superb view of Long Row, Upper Race, provides an excellent picture of early nineteenth-century workers' accommodation. These rather primitive cottages by today's standards, were previously named 'New Row' and due to their close proximity to the various industrial workings, were often in a much-overcrowded state. Partly confirming this, the reverse of this picture postcard from 1908, bears a message from the sender stating that eleven members of his family may be seen amongst the inhabitants on the photograph!

CHAPTER 2

Pontypool's Near Neighbours

54. Moving on to one of Pontypool's near neighbours and this view is looking down a 'traffic-free' main road through New Inn almost ninety years ago. Some local lads stand for the cameraman, he being positioned outside the Council School which is just out of the picture to the left. Now closed as a school, the building has found a new lease of life as a Family Learning Centre.

55. Another early scene at New Inn, this time from outside the old Rising Sun Inn which is on the left and seen before its transformation into more up-to-date premises. On the opposite side of the road, the milk cart standing outside the village coal yard belongs to one of the district's farmers - Henry Harris of New House Farm, Panteg.

56. Facing in the opposite direction towards New Inn's shopping centre in about 1910, provides an opportunity to recall a former hostelry, the Pineapple Inn, seen in the middle of the picture. This public house was demolished a few decades ago and replaced by a block of four flats; the old stone-built wall opposite has also been removed, the site now being occupied by a local paint supplier and car sales forecourt.

57. Compared to many of the photographs included in the book, this particular one is relatively modern - the Highway, New Inn during the early 1960s and yet there are numerous changes to take note of. On the extreme left, the grocery shop belonging to A.A. Watkins is now the premises of the Condensation Centre and, some further alteration has taken place next door, with the house since demolished to make way for the roadway leading to Afon Close. Further along in the next block, the small store displaying the *'Spar'* sign is now the local fish and chip shop.

58. Today's residents of New Inn will find this view from about 1906 a much-changed and perhaps unrecognisable scene, with new housing now taking up the vast majority of the once-green pasture. As a guide to the precise location, the houses nearest form part of Prospect Place and, in the right background, displaying its former bell tower, is New Inn's mixed school, first erected in 1893 and enlarged in 1907 to cater for the fast-growing pupil population.

59. Having proceeded just a mile or two to the east of New Inn, the photograph is of the main highway from Pontypool to Usk and Abergavenny. This is how the original Usk Road looked in the 1930s, a time when it ran directly alongside that well-patronised public house, The Wain-y-Clare at Cwmoody. For historians of beer and its makers, it will be noted that this pub at the time was selling Phillips Ales and Stouts. An ancient brewer of Newport (founded in 1874), it was a popular supplier to the trade before being taken over by the much larger company, Simmonds in 1949.

60. Back to New Inn, and a military parade through the centre of the village in about 1908. Whilst it has attracted a large crowd onto the street, the precise reason for such an ensemble is unknown. The houses in the background belong to *'Mary Ann Terrace'*, addressed nowadays as the Highway; the hardware shop, near right now forms part of the 'Spar' store.

61. Crossing over the Afon Llwyd river to Griffithstown, the picture is of its main shopping area in Windsor Road. The butcher's shop of John Fairfax is just visible on the extreme left and further along, the nearest building with the upper bay windows is the site of the local post office, it having moved from its original position just past where the horse and cart are standing. Although the frontage has altered somewhat over the years, this long-standing office remains on the same spot as it did in this photograph from 1912.

62. A peaceful-looking High Street in the year 1905, the street having changed from its original name of Cross Street, given in the latter half of the nineteenth century. The butcher's shop on the left, was one of seven trading in Griffithstown at the time and belonged to Mr. Robert Thomas Bach, he moving to more central premises in Windsor Road a few years later.

63. The sturdy houses of Charles Street are seen here during the early years of the twentieth century. The development of Charles Street was assisted by a small Building Society known as *'The Griffithstown Building Club'*, an association which was formed in 1890 by a few local gentlemen who shared a common interest in creating modern and quality-built houses for local residents of the district.

64. Asquith Street's well-dressed children, in their period clothing, are pictured in 1907 from the junction with Edward Street. It is noticeable that the houses built here are somewhat similar in design to those in Charles Street, suggesting further involvement of the aforementioned local building society. The name *'Asquith'* was probably adopted from the eminent Liberal politician and Prime Minister, Herbert Henry Asquith who took office in 1908 shortly after this photograph.

65. The upper part of Kemys Street as it appeared in 1906 at the crossroads with Florence Place on the extreme left, and Oxford Street opposite, where the shop of Mrs. Ann Fisher is seen at number one. Much of Kemys Street, as well as portions of other streets leading off, were constructed around the year 1875 on land leased from Mr. Sampson Copestake, founder of the local steelworks in 1873.

66. Some young ladies of Florence Place catch the photographer's eye when pictured in this early scene. As mentioned in the previous photograph, Florence Place is one such street leading off from Kemys Street and is shown above, before its completion, an additional six houses being built later on the far left. On the right hand side, the nearest six houses to the camera were the first to be constructed - they appearing on an 1882 map of the district.

67. An impressive picture postcard view of Cambria Street from 1907, when most of the children in the near vicinity appear to have gathered to pose for the photographer. The slate-covered houses on the immediate right, together with the following three blocks which include Oak Place and Cambria Terrace (dated 1871), were the first to be erected. More housing was to follow further along the right hand side including Scarboro (sic) Terrace dating from 1889.

Old Bakehouse Publications

Order from your Bookseller or direct from

The Old Bakehouse
Church Street
Abertillery
Gwent NP13 1EA
Tel: 01495 212600
Fax: 01495 216222

68. Another scene at Windsor Road almost ninety-five years ago and this time looking downwards. Situated between the first two buildings on the immediate right is a narrow lane leading onto Queen Street, and although presently unoccupied, this is where the premises of number 53 now stand. On the opposite side of the road, to what has now become Griffithstown's permanent post office, is a much-overladen horse and cart delivering some of the local residents' needs.

69. Quiet times in Commercial Street are reflected in this picture from 1906. The block of five houses on the immediate right, known originally as *'Holiday Terrace'* and now numbered 86-90, were built on a plot of land purchased by Mr. John Watkin, the G.W.R. locomotive superintendent at Pontypool Road in about 1870. The name *'Holiday Terrace'* is visible on the façade of the houses above the bushes but was obscured during re-decorations in the 1950s. In the next block, some of Griffithstown's trading places may be seen, the nearest shop belonging to Mrs. Catherine Williams at number 85 and, further along at the far end, at number 80, is the business of boot and shoe dealer and coal merchant, William Frederick Sumner.

70. This scene is photographed in the direction of Coed-y-Gric Institution from the former stone-built viaduct that carried the roadway from Griffithstown to New Inn. The viaduct spanned the vast railway complex at Pontypool Road, the buildings on either side being the carriage and wagon sheds. The bridge, which stood for more than a hundred years, was eventually demolished to make way for the present-day bypass.

71. The Monmouthshire Canal, where it lies between Commercial Street and Station Road is a temptation for some local boys to take 'a dip' during the summer of 1908. The canal, once used for the transportation of minerals from the valley's industries was by now, in a state of deterioration and at the time, it may not have been too healthy a venue for a swim.

72. A view that overlooks the upper part of Griffithstown shows Mountain Lane leading onto Sunnybank Road. The large house just to the right of the lane and known as *'The Cedars'*, was constructed by a Mrs. Bell during the period of the building of St. Hilda's Church. The reported intention was that *'The Cedars'* would become the vicarage for St. Hilda's but, for some reason this did not materialise and the lady took up residence herself. The much older structure in the foreground, known as *'Sunnybank Cottage'*, was extended and completely renovated in the 1970s, thus making it almost unrecognisable nowadays when compared to this original photograph from about 1914.

73. An early twentieth-century view of Sunnybank Road looking south, with St. Hilda's Church in the distance. Originally known as Church Road when the photograph was taken, the development of this thoroughfare commenced in the early 1890s, eventually leading to widening and surface improvement throughout its entire length. It was almost twenty years after construction had first begun before the new name of Sunnybank was adopted.

74. Sunnybank Road is again featured in this general view from the 1920s and illustrates that by now, Griffithstown had become quite a well-developed area. To the right of the picture and leading off from Sunnybank Road, are the houses that form part of Mary Street (now known as St. Mary's Street) - dwellings that started to appear in the 1890s. In the distance the extensive Panteg Works, with its numerous smoke stacks may also be seen.

75. Captioned '*A Peep at Griffithstown*', this picture-postcard scene overlooks Cwrdy Road during the late 1920s, with the former ancient building of Cwrdy Farm left of centre. The farmhouse, believed to date from the sixteenth century is also thought to have once held the Llanfrechfa Parish meetings, its name '*Cwrdy*' probably originating from the Welsh - '*Cwrdd*' (meeting) and '*Dy*' for '*Ty*' (house). The Williams family occupied the farm for at least three generations until the 1960s, when it was finally demolished leaving little trace except for part of a wall. Around the time of its demise, housing development had already started and now completely covers the site.

76. This imposing and scarce photograph, consisting of a block of ten houses may, at first glance give the reader a problem in locating the precise whereabouts. Situated in Stafford Road and now numbered 41 to 59 (odd numbers only), it lies just south of Griffithstown's well-known 'spout'; its former nineteenth-century name being 'Hanbury Terrace' or 'Club Row'. The houses, which are pre 1886, are pictured here in about 1906, the frontage appearing to be quite perilous for the inhabitants, the roadway having since been built up considerably in later years.

77. The lower end of South Street, Sebastopol at the junction with Sherbourne Road in about 1912. The prominent store on the corner is the grocery shop of Mr. E. Cleaves and Son, a family business that traded in the village for many years. Next door, where the lady and gentleman are stood at the doorway, is another of Sebastopol's long-standing businesses, the property of eminent shopkeeper Mr. Robert Whatmore. Looking further along and to the left of the picture, the Penry Memorial Chapel, built some twenty years previous in 1893 may be seen.

78. The canal at Sebastopol during the 1960s, is pictured from the Crown Bridge as a pleasure boat, heading towards Griffithstown, passes by St. Oswald's Church. The bridge, which through the campaigning by Torfaen Canal Society and volunteers from the Inland Waterways Association and Canal Trust, succeeded in their endeavours when eventually, the bridge was raised in 1994 to allow boats to pass safely through.

79. Pictured in 1912 from just above the Old Crown Inn, this nostalgic look at some of Sebastopol's former dwellings is sure to revive a few memories of some of its residents. The group of cottages situated on Greenhill Road which are believed to date from the mid 1850s, survived until a few decades ago. The entrance to the lane on the extreme right, led to the rear of Woodland Terrace, yet another name from yesteryear. This terrace stood between the cottages and a block of three nearby houses, of which the lone survivor is these days a popular Fish and Chip shop.

CHAPTER 3

Local People, Places & Events

80. The location for this daredevil stunt on Whitsun Tuesday 1903 is Pontypool Park, then in the ownership of the Hanbury family. The performer, who goes by the name of *'Giffon'* is seen doing the high dive from a structure 60 to 70 feet in height, accordingly described by the sender of this picture postcard. Although the objective of the dive is uncertain, Giffon can be seen leaving the structure on a bicycle, probably hoping to land in a tank of water.

81. The Polo Grounds at New Inn, where many events were held before the local authorities acquired Pontypool Park from the Hanbury family shortly after World War One. It appears that the arena is being prepared for a Bank Holiday event, with the structure on the right being very similar to that in the previous photograph.

82. A photograph from August 1907 during a rifle-shooting competition held at Mill Field Pontnewynydd. The two most successful of the local competitors at the open-air range, which was organised by the Welsh Miniature Rifle Association, were Captain A. Sale and Private A.E. Morton. Pictured above are some of the entrants in the 25-yard range.

83. Members of the Pontypool and District Ambulance Corps display their trophies which were won during 1916-17 and their names, pictured left to right are - Back Row: Pte. W.J. Harris, Pte. J. Thomas, Corps Supt. A.J. England, Supt. of stores R.T. Davies, Sgt. C. Thomas and Pte. H. Harris. Front: Sgt. T. Miles, Pte. R.L. Jones, Div. Supt. G.H. Nelms, Dr. R.W. Haslett, Cpl. W. Meredith, Cpl. C. Bullock and Sgt. E. Webster.

84. This photograph, taken outside Pontymoile park gates during the 1930s, presents a little mystery, as the occasion and who the gentlemen actually are (except one) remain unknown. The one gent positively identified is Mr. Frank Luxton (stood eighth from the left), who lived at Charlesville Pontnewynydd and worked for the General Post Office.

85. In August 1924, and for the first time in its history, the honour came to Pontypool in welcoming the Royal National Eisteddfod of Wales. This was an honour that was greatly appreciated not only by the inhabitants of the town, but also by the many people of Monmouthshire. The advertising card published to promote the event and seen opposite, well- illustrates that all roads led to Pontypool.

YN WYNEB HAUL ||| LLYGAD GOLEUNI

ROYAL NATIONAL EISTEDDFOD
OF
WALES

AUGUST: 4,5,6,7,8,9.

ANTON EDWARDS

PONTYPOOL

Privy Purse Office,
Buckingham Palace, S.W.
3rd January 1923.

Dear Sir,

In reply to your letter of the 22nd ult., addressed to the King, I am commanded to inform you that His Majesty is graciously pleased to grant his Patronage to the National Eisteddfod of Wales, which will be held at Pontypool in August 1924.

Yours faithfully,
F. M. PONSONBY,
Keeper of the Privy Purse.

R. Stephen, Esq.,
1, Victoria Road,
Pontypool.

86. A scene from the National Eisteddfod week at the terrace entrance to the Italian Gardens. Two young ladies in appropriate Welsh costume are seen on the steps, and to the left, behind the ornamental railings, some of the many flags that decorated the town are in sight.

87. Another scene from the 1924 Eisteddfod and such an event in the Welsh calendar would not be complete without a most distinguished visitor. Wearing a bowler hat and sporting an umbrella is H.R.H. the Prince of Wales, Prince Edward as he inspects the guard of honour provided by ex-servicemen under the command of J.O. Tyler who is seen talking to the prince. Also in attendance are Lord Treowen (left) and Mr. D.C. Udell on the right.

Cyflwynwyd y Gadair gan Gwmni y County Furnishing, Pont-y-pwl.
Cynlluniwyd gan Kelt Edwards, Ysw.

Chair presented by the County Furnishing Company, Pontypool.
Designed by Kelt Edwards, Esq.

88. The Bardic chair for the Eisteddfod was made and presented by the popular and long-established furniture retailer of the town, The County Furnishing Co. as illustrated in this advertisement.

89. June 2nd 1953 saw the coronation of Her Majesty Queen Elizabeth II and the occasion is being celebrated with a street party here in Capel Street Pontypool. Amongst the crowd some names to recall are Les Dobbs, Ethel Dobbs, Mr. Powell, Joan Smith, Phyllis Probert, Vera Evans, Vic Evans, Terry Warwood and Mr. and Mrs. Warwood.

90. Another street party, this time it is being held in St. Cadoc's Road Trevethin to celebrate the 1951 Festival of Britain. The ladies, seen left to right are - Mrs. Olwen Owen, Mrs. Flo Tudgay, Mrs. Ivy Aston, Mrs. Cathy Jayne, Mrs. Vi Harris, Mrs. Marge Pearce, Mrs. May Betts, Mrs. Peggy Gillum, Pauline Betts, Mrs. Hilda Groves and Mrs. Kate Hughes; the lad in the front is a very young Keith Aston.

91. The residents of Picton Street, Griffithstown celebrate one of the great events of the twentieth century, V.E. Day May 8th 1945 when almost six years of war in Europe came to an end. Unfortunately space does not allow for the naming of the collection of faces seen here although undoubtedly, many will be very familiar to local residents.

92. A gathering of residents of Old Penygarn pose for a photograph outside the house *'Glenvellyn'* in the 1950s, whilst the occasion is uncertain here are their names. The three gentlemen are Trevor Lloyd (left), Bert Jenkins (back) and Jack Winterhalter (right). The ladies, positioned approximately left to right, starting at the back are Gwen Thomas, Dorothy Evans, Hilda Morgan, Evadne Wood, Mrs. Evans, Marjorie Mansell, Mary (nee Griffiths), Kay Gunne, Miss Protheroe, Ruth Williams, Mrs. Knipe, Mrs. Schofield, Dorothy Griffiths, Peggy Moseley, Eileen Winterhalter, Cissy Lloyd but regrettably the author has been unable to trace the name of the lady sat next to Jack Winterhalter.

93. A large assembly of Panteg Hospital staff and their families pictured at St. Hilda's church hall for the annual dance in about 1948-49. The photograph, taken more than fifty years ago, is guaranteed to remind some readers of friends and relatives who were in attendance.

94. A most popular venue for parties and various functions was Pontypool's Clarence Hotel, and some of the catering staff are seen here taking a short break from their duties during a wedding reception in the 1950s. Regrettably, the author has been able to trace two names only - Elaine Paget (extreme left) and Ivy Luxton (4th from left) who was the hotel's principal cook.

95. More celebrations are underway during the 1950s, this time at Lower Mill Row, Pontymoile. Originally built for workers at the nearby Lower Mills Works, the row, which was demolished in the 1960s consisted of about fifteen houses. Immediately opposite the cottages, may be seen some of the primitive outside toilets, each one having to serve two households! Some of the ladies pictured here are, from the nearest left - Mrs. Purnell, Elsie Bennett, Kathy Appleton, Mrs. Haddock and Adelaide Johnson. Nearest right - Mrs. Ormond, unknown and Y. McGuire. In the background is a former industrial landmark, the water tower belonging to Pilkington's glassworks.

96. A photograph from 1938 during the opening of the St. John Ambulance Brigade hall on Hospital Road, built for the Pontnewynydd Division and replacing its previous venue at Zion Hill Junior School. A few names have been traced amongst the group and they are - Mr. Pope, Supt. Ted Webster, Tom Mason, Mrs. B. Harding, Vera Griffiths, Mrs. Smith, Mabess Templar, N/Supt. Florence Dukes and Mrs. Bassett.

97. The visit by British air heroine Amy Johnson was the highlight of the 1936 Pontypool Hospital Carnival. Born in Hull in 1904, Amy Johnson made solo flights to Australia in 1930 and to The Cape and back during this 1936 carnival year. She died at an early age when, in 1941 her plane, an air transport auxiliary was lost over the Thames estuary. Amy and her husband Jim Mollison are stood either side of carnival queen Myra James in the above photograph. Many other well-known celebrities were invited to help boost the attendances during hospital carnival years, amongst whom were world renowned boxers Tommy Farr and Freddie Mills. Inaugurated by Pontypool Chamber of Trade in 1929, hospital carnival day was always guaranteed to attract vast crowds, not just from Pontypool and nearby villages but from numerous other valley towns, with the 1930s being the heyday of carnival tradition. Any profits gained during the week were used in the upkeep of Pontypool hospital, so vital during this period when unemployment in the district was at unprecedented levels and voluntary contributions were dramatically reduced. There being no National Health Service functioning at the time, hospital treatment for those out of work and their families relied so heavily on the generosity of those supporters of Pontypool hospital, particularly its annual carnival.

98. This picture, taken in the grounds of Pontypool hospital is a gathering of some nursing staff and local dignitaries. The occasion is thought to be the opening of the new three-storey wing in 1928. Amongst the dignitaries is Mr. Benjamin Nicholas J.P. who is stood in the back row. He was a native of Ruabon but became a prominent figure in the industrial life of south Wales, with particular interests in the Pontypool district, he serving as managing director of Tirpentwys Colliery for 45 years. Mr. Nicholas died at Osborne House on his 81st birthday in 1933.

99. This is a group of Belgian soldiers at the hospital seen during a period of treatment for their injuries received on the battlefields of World War One 1914-1918. Their country, completely overrun by the German forces, meant wounded troops having to be shipped to the United Kingdom and a number of local hospitals were to play an important part in their recovery.

100. Another scene at the hospital from more recent times, around 1950-51 as patients and staff enjoy some sunshine and a breath of fresh air. Unfortunately only two names from the group have been traced and they are - Mr. Vic Evans (standing 2nd from left at the front) and Madge Fynn (sitting 5th from the left).

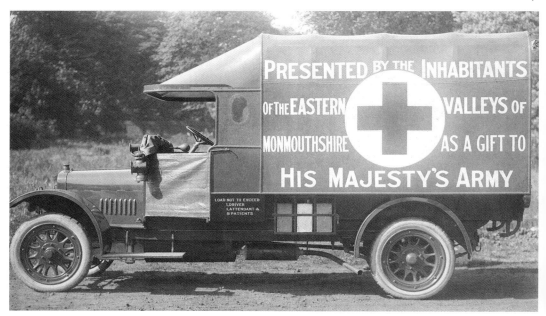

101. This First World War Sunbeam ambulance was subscribed for by the people of the eastern valley for the war effort in 1915 at a cost of £460. Before being handed over by Mr. W.C. Watkins to Colonel Hepburn, who was representing Sir Henry McKinnon G.O.C. Western Command, the vehicle was ceremoniously driven through the streets of Pontypool. Some details on the side of the ambulance state *'Load not to exceed 1 driver, 1 attendant and 8 patients'*.

102. From the Second World War years is a photograph of some members of the Auxiliary Fire Service based at Griffithstown, their meeting places being an off-licence in Kemys Street and a building in Park Street, now occupied by an engineering company. Most of the gentlemen can be named as follows, left to right - Back: Cliff Stevens, Mr. Lewis, ?, ?, Lester Price, Dai Davies and Jack Ingram. Third Row: Doc Woodman, Eddie Bevan, ?, Frank Parry, Bill Watkins, ? , Joe Wilcox and Fred Ellaway Second Row: Eddie Bissex, ?, Mr. Wilkie, Mr. Kimton, Bill Hughes, and Mr. Davies. Front: Derrick Hall, Melvin Hall, Clifford Cox, Chester Jones and Mr. Foster. The trophy held by Mr. Cox was won in a challenge cup competition at Pontypool Park after beating Abergavenny in the final.

103. Some members of Griffithstown's Home Guard, a voluntary part-time military force organised nationwide in 1940 to assist in the country's defence against possible invasion. The Griffithstown H.Q. was at the local Drill Hall and a few names have been identified as follows - Danny Williams (back row 2nd left), Glyn Davies (back row 6th left). Front: Unknown, unknown, Horace Thomas, Mr. Wilcox, Frank Reynolds, Mr. Britton and Arthur Adams.

104. Fifty officers and constables belonging to the Monmouthshire Constabulary, Pontypool Division, are pictured at the rear of the County Court and Police Station in May, 1931. The premises, rebuilt and enlarged some twenty years previous was, by the 1950s proving inadequate and thus new and more spacious Headquarters and County Court were subsequently constructed.

105. In early 1959 the estimated cost of providing new premises was given as £86,000 and the building is pictured above, shortly after opening (the year 1962 may be seen inscribed at the top of each drainpipe). Also in the picture some former structures are to be noted. On the extreme left, at the site of today's top car park, is the old Crane Street station goods shed and to the right of the police station, the rear of the Wheatsheaf public house is just visible at the top end of Market Street.

CHAPTER 4

Trading Places

106. The original George Hotel in Commercial Street Pontypool as photographed in the year 1868, the corner of the façade being occupied by a watchmaker and jeweller's shop. In later years, the building lost its decorative appearance and the corner of the shop became the entrance to the hotel, this being prior to 1905 when the George was completely altered to the semblance of today. Next door, the Greyhound Hotel has also seen major alterations since being pictured here more than 130 years ago.

107. One of Pontypool's numerous grocery shops before the arrival of the supermarket was the Star Supply Stores, originally known as the Star Tea Company during the early 1900s. This long-established business was situated at number 19 George Street and served customers of the town until the early 1960s when it finally closed. These premises are nowadays occupied by a travel agency.

108. Mr. Alwyn Morgan, a disabled soldier from the 1914-18 war stands outside his boot shop at number 75 George Street Pontypool, and the sign in his window states that *'all work is executed under personal supervision and only experienced workmen employed'*. Now demolished, the premises may be better remembered in later years by the more mature town shopper as a pet shop.

109. The premises of William Henry Pegington of Pontnewynydd in about 1904, one of two such butcher's shops trading in Hanbury Road at the time; the other being Hedley Weeks. The young lad on the doorstep is thought to be Cyril Arthur Pegington, eldest son of William Henry who, by the late 1920s had taken over the business from his father. Mr. Pegington senior, had by then moved on to Glascoed, having bought 'Hill Farm'. The shop premises still survives as a private dwelling and is appropriately called 'The Old Butcher's Shop'.

110. The location for this superb photograph featuring two modes of early transport belonging to John Basil Jenkins and Son, is the canal bank at Sebastopol. The premises for this family business of grocers and bakers was built in 1874, and is pictured along with its staff during the 1920s, next to the older adjoining Panteg Hotel (formerly the Shearers Arms). The frontage of the shop has since changed totally to form part of its present occupants, Panteg Nursing Home.

111. The former corner shop at the junction of High Street and Commercial Street Griffithstown which belonged to the Lewis family. Stood in the doorway is Margaret Lewis in whose name the business was registered, with husband William standing by the firm's van during the 1930s. As can be seen from the front of the shop with its numerous signs, the family were purveyors of cigarettes and tobacco but were also advertising in the traders' directory as 'Refreshment Rooms, No.1 High Street'. The building has in recent times been converted into a number of flats.

112. In the doorway of his outfitter's shop at No.65a Commercial Street, is another of Griffithstown's tradesmen, Mr. Arthur Beynon. The shop which was previously Henry Peach's grocery and drapery store and afterwards Joseph Caswell's chemist, developed in a room at No.65. After seeing use as an outfitter's, the premises were subsequently acquired by a local barber.

113. One of the longest-surviving shops in Pontypool is Woolworth's, the company having traded from the same building (somewhat modernised) since 1923. This is a photograph of the management and staff seen outside the store in the 1950s.

114. One favourite eating-place in Pontypool from years gone by, was the faggot and pea stall situated at the top end of the market hall. The café is shown in 1951 during the Festival of Britain celebrations with owners Gordon and Doris Albert facing the camera. Gordon stands in front of the counter, Doris is just behind the glass cabinet and their assistant Eunice is in the centre.

ANN'S PANTRY
F. A. AMPHLETT & SONS   EST. 1920

COOKED MEAT MANUFACTURERS

PERSONAL SUPERVISION
SAFEGUARDS OUR
REPUTATION

at

THE MODEL COOKED MEAT FACTORY
WAINFELIN RD.   Phone 335   PONTYPOOL

also

8, 9 & 10 — — THE MARKET

115. 'Ann's Pantry' was another former family business in Pontypool market. The firm founded in 1920 by Flora Ann Amphlett, finally closed in the early 1990s after more than seventy years of trading. Brothers Roger and Richard Amphlett, who took over the business in 1959, believed the combined effects of recession, poor car-parking and 'out of town' shopping, (a not unfamiliar observation from the traders of the town), led to eventual closure. The picture above dates from more prosperous times in 1953 and behind the counter, left to right, are Dave Amphlett, Bill Symes, Tony Amphlett and Bill Thomas.

116. Pontnewynydd's post office staff pictured in about 1912, an era when a letter could be posted for a mere halfpenny. The office which had moved from nearby Hanbury Road in the early 1900s was by now, situated in St. Luke's Road. The sub-postmistress Mrs. Mary B. Whittington who, with her husband Mr. Walter H. Whittington also ran a tobacconist and newsagent business from the same premises. The couple are believed to be the two elderly persons pictured in the front of the photograph.

117. Pontypool's Hanbury Hotel at the corner of Clarence Street and Trosnant Street, which is one of the town's well-established licensed premises still offering its services today. The hotel was undoubtedly so-named after the family who brought fame and prosperity to the district through the manufacture of iron, tin and wire. It is pictured here with some of its regulars in about 1906 when Mr. Robert Shutt was the proprietor.

118. Decorated for the 1953 coronation celebrations, is the 'Labour In Vain', an inn originally known as the Jolly Colliers and sited on the Sow Hill. The name 'Sow Hill' derives from an era when mules carried the 'sows' and 'pigs' (casts of iron) from the Cwm Glyn furnaces to the Osborne and Park forges, via High Street and Crane Street. Stood on the doorstep are licensees Mr. and Mrs. Brown who took over in 1946 having succeeded Mrs. Brown's parents, Mr. and Mrs. Fred Harvey who had been 'pulling pints' there since 1928. The old pub sign that hung outside for many years, portraying a woman leaning over a tub attempting to wash clean (and white), a coloured boy was replaced in later years reportedly in response to racial criticism.

119. Yet another of the area's public houses, the Lower New Inn, seen here in Edwardian times displaying an advertisement for the now-defunct Phillips Ales. The cottage, adjacent to this old staging post inn for coaches, has long been demolished, together with a number of others which are out of view and also a blacksmith's shop which stood at the rear.

120./121. Two surviving photographs illustrating the countless changes that have occurred at Pontymoile during the past few decades. The Hanbury Farmhouse Bread Bakery that once stood opposite the old Pontymoile Mission and adjacent to Panteg Council Offices, is pictured from the railway bridge that used to span the main road to Griffithstown. Below, the cameraman has been allowed inside the bakery to photograph the ovens and both pictures date from 1906, when the business was under the ownership of William Jones and Company. Many readers may remember that in later years, the building was occupied by Ruther's, fruit, vegetable and fish merchant warehouse. Further use of part of the building was also made by the West Mon Old Boys Association.

122. The Cwmffrwdoer branch of the Abersychan, Talywain and British Co-operative Society dated 1903 and which opened in 1906. The store, sited at Hanbury Road Pontnewynydd, was originally the freehold shop premises of grocer and ironmonger Mr. Thomas Williams. Upon purchase of the shop by the Society, additions and alterations were made to make it suitable for the Co-op trade, and two years later an extension was added. Further extensions were made in the 1930s to meet the growing trade of this once-popular branch. The building still stands today, although at the time of publication, it lies vacant.

123. A later No.4 branch (seen above) of the Abersychan Co-op was opened at Albion Road, Pontypool in March 1916, despite the Society experiencing great trading difficulties during the war years. The official opening was performed by the president, Mr. W.H. Blackmore and the duties of branch manager were entrusted to Mr. R.J. Connop who had been employed by the Society since March 1905. However, the opening of a new Co-op shop at the former Café Royal in Pontypool town centre, in May 1933, brought about the closure of the Albion Road branch soon afterwards; the Co-operative subsequently converted the building into a dairy.

CHAPTER 5

Places of Worship & Learning

124. Mount Pleasant Church strategically situated in Hanbury Road Pontypool, seen just a few years after its opening in 1905. The foundation stones for the church and schoolrooms were first laid in 1903, the total cost estimated to ultimately exceed some £6,000. This place of worship was constructed as a replacement for the original Mount Pleasant, which had stood in Nicholas Street since 1855 and after fifty years of strong independent following, had become quite inadequate.

125. The ancient Baptist Chapel at Penygarn, the formation of which began in the year 1726. A centre of nonconformist worship at the time was in the Trosnant district, with visiting preachers from afar coming to support the cause. Early meetings were held in local private dwellings, with baptisms performed in Trosnant meadow near the Afon Llwyd. By 1726 it was evident that a more permanent meeting place was urgently needed by followers of independent faith, and a site on Penygarn Hill was secured, the chapel opening some twelve months later. The first pastor was a young and forceful man by the name of Miles Harry who served Penygarn for a remarkable forty-one years and did much to further the Cause in Monmouthshire.

126. Trevethin Parish Church Institute, situated in Osborne Road, which was acquired by the church in 1916 from the Junior Conservative Club for use as a centre for social activities and a Sunday School. The building, seen here in 1934, was converted into a cinema in 1974 after the town's last picture house, the Park Cinema, was destroyed by fire in 1970.

127. Griffithstown Baptist Church, which like a number of others in the district, developed from an already existing preaching centre. The latter half of the nineteenth century was a period of development and population growth in the town, and many worshippers were still making their way to Pontypool for Baptist services. In 1875 four members of Zion Chapel, Lower Trosnant voiced their opinion that Griffithstown was long overdue for a mission of its own and subsequently the church agreed to support the request. The first services were actually held in the Mechanics Institute before the permanent building was opened in 1878.

128. The introductory years of pastorship at Griffithstown Baptist were unsettled ones, the first minister being Rev. Joseph Tucker, a former railway worker from Glascoed. Rev. Tucker did well in swelling the numbers in his congregation until sudden departure, for uncertain reasons, thereby causing a most severe decline. His successor, Mr. David Morgan Davies fared no better and the church was said to be in the doldrums until the arrival in 1897, of the gentleman seen in this picture, J. Howell Rees of Pembrokeshire. Mr. Rees's pastorate was seen as the turning point for the church, he being responsible for the restoration of unity, congregation numbers and financial stability. In 1904 he launched an expansion programme which included the addition of galleries, a lecture hall and a suite of classrooms. The church was saddened when in 1908, after so much hard work at Griffithstown, he decided to accept a call from Counterslip Baptist Church, Bristol.

129. St. John's Church Wainfelin with the houses of Bushy Park in the background. St. John's may be considered quite a young building, compared to many other places of worship in the Pontypool district. Construction began in 1912, when the ground was kindly donated by the proprietor of the town's most prestigious shop, Mr. Edwin Fowler. The official opening took place in September 1913 with further extensions to the church completed in 1926

130. This picture presents a rare opportunity to see the interior of St. John's, and although the author has been unable to trace the many names of the choir and church members, their faces will surely be very familiar to many readers of this book. However a few to look out for are Charlie Watkins, Billy Smith, Mrs. Dennis (Sunday School Teacher) and Mrs. Rowles.

131. Another interior photograph from St. John's, and on this occasion the members appear to be gathered in the crypt for an important feast. Again, not many names have come to light other than Mrs. Mary Smith, Billy Smith and Edgar Smith.

132. St. David's Presbyterian was a well-known and well-supported church in Osborne Road for generations until it suffered the all too familiar fate of gradual lack of congregations. Opened in 1905, this picture was taken just a few years later and shows the pastor at the time, Rev. W.D.O. Jones (centre) surrounded by some of his flock; St. David's closed in 1991 and nowadays stands as a block of flats.

133. Llanvihangel Church, Pontymoile which is dedicated to St. Michael, was mentioned in the Norwich Taxation of 1291 when its value was given at forty shillings (£2) and at the time, was assigned to the Prioress of Usk. The church is seen here in about 1910, having been completely rebuilt in 1736, with the Welsh tongue being the only language preached and understood until the latter end of the nineteenth century.

134. New Inn Chapel as it looked some ninety years ago. This chapel was the leading place for the nonconformists of New Inn, the movement having been fashionable in the area since the seventeenth century. Early religious meetings took place in a private dwelling called 'Newydd' which was acquired in about 1740 and were to continue as such, for almost a century and a half before the building seen in this picture was opened in 1884.

135. A photograph taken outside St. Alban's Catholic Church in the early years of the twentieth century. At the entrance is Father Peter Degan who was cleric in charge for a remarkable twenty-five years until he passed away in 1915.

136. St. Hilda's Church Griffithstown, an institution in the town since 1888. This picture which was taken outside the church hall in about 1930, shows the former 'Girls Friendly Society' (accompanied by some boys) apparently in fancy dress mode.

137. Upper Trosnant Baptist Church, yet another house of ancient prayers in Pontypool. Trosnant Church found its origins in a private house called 'The Wern' owned by a Mr. Miles Edwards of Panteg who until 1776, had been a faithful member of Penygarn Baptist until a 'rift' caused him and a number of others to go their separate ways. Miles Edwards and his followers soon established themselves and managed to purchase a house in Upper Trosnant for £252 in 1779, converting it into their first chapel with Mr. Edwards serving as minister until his death in 1808. By 1820, the movement was flourishing with sufficient funds available to erect a new chapel now under the pastorship of Mr. John Williams. Subsequent alterations and renovations have taken place over the years, but the chapel is one of the few survivors of religious following in Pontypool.

138. Now demolished, this is the old Trosnant College which was founded in 1736 and situated near the Baptist Chapel and adjoining churchyard. Led by Miles Harry and his associates at Penygarn, the old college building was responsible for the teaching of innumerable local preachers, many of whom carried their religious knowledge to England, Ireland and even the United States.

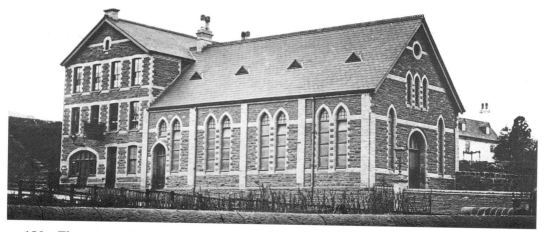

139. The new and yet much-needed reshaping of the town's road system during the late 1990s, particularly at Pontymoile, led to the removal of a number of former landmarks. One for example was the Mission Hall, seen here some ninety years earlier having been opened in 1891 for Christian worship and a place of refuge and salvation for those who might have 'gone astray'. Fortunately a completely new replacement building can now be found a short distance away.

140. A picturesque view of St. Mary's Church, Panteg which was taken many years ago. Its origins can be traced back to the thirteenth century at the very least, with mention being made in the Taxation of 1254 that Panteg Church was 'too poor to be taxed'. The Register however does not appear to have been commenced until 1598, but was maintained unbroken thereafter except for a period during the Civil War. This was a time when marauding Parliamentary troops plundered the church, its ancient bells and even the burial ground, but failed to locate the whereabouts of the vital church records. St. Mary's was to remain the parish church for Panteg, New Inn and Sebastopol until the establishment of St. Hilda's in Griffithstown, which then went on to absorb part of Panteg and Trevethin within its boundaries by 1898.

141. In the background of this early picture which overlooks Freeholdland, may be seen the Pontnewynydd Board School, as it was then known, the school having opened in Lower Leigh Road in 1901. The original Snatchwood Church School, built in 1845, stood on the other side of the valley, it closing as the new one opened, then to be used as a church hall and Sunday School.

142. A traditional school photograph taken at Snatchwood School in about 1965; regrettably space does not permit the listing of names but the pupils, who would now be in their 'forties', may well recognise themselves and some old school friends.

143. This time its the turn of the girls at the County Grammar School, Pontypool to be seen in full song. The occasion is thought to be a prize-giving day during the 1950s and at the piano is the unmistakable Professor Alfred Thompson.

144. Some thirty years on from the previous photograph and the school has now changed its name to Trevethin Comprehensive and opened its doors to male pupils as well as girls. This picture is of a member of staff and Form 4X in 1983.

145. Pupils are seen exercising in the yard of Griffithstown School, Park Street in the early 1900s. This school was built in 1874 for a mixed pupillage of 300, it being enlarged in 1904 to cater for 434 children when responsibility passed to the County Council. At the time of this photograph the headmaster was Mr. Thomas R.Wigley who served the same school for an incredible 41 years.

146. A picture which has the original caption 'Little Welsh Lasses - Griffithstown Infant School, March 1911 - St. David's Day'. As the town developed and expanded through the latter years of the nineteenth century, little thought was given to the need for a local school, with children having to travel to Wern, Sebastopol and Pontymoile. When Griffithstown School was opened in 1874, it was still under the jurisdiction of Llanfrechfa Parish with much wrangling on decision-making until attaining its own school board in 1889. Some interesting statistics from the period reveal that the starting age was three and pupils could leave as early as twelve years.

147. A scene at Wern School in about 1960 and the ladies more than likely form a group of netball players. In the picture and left to right are - Back: Susan Haycock, Elaine Baddeley, Susan Willets, Kay Bridgeman, Heather Manley, Barbara Connick, Jennifer Morgan and teacher Miss Davies. Seated: Andrea Critchley, Gwen Ferris, Susan Lewis and Sandra Evans. Front: Josie Thomas.

148. A picture of some pride at George Street Council School during the 1930s when four pupils were each presented with a watch, awarded by Monmouthshire Education Authority for five years regular attendance. The boys, left to right are - George Pearce, Aubrey Cox, Herbert Evans and James Hawes. The head teachers are Mr. John Thomas and Miss H. Fletcher.

149. This is a group of pupils belonging to Park Terrace School in about 1920 and a few names have been traced as follows, reading left to right - Back: Bertie Calton, Mervyn Cottrell and Billy Williams (2, 3, 4), Herbert Tibbs (6), Dennis Pocock (10). Middle: Grace Curzon (2). Front: Violet Haynes, Ada Griffiths, Lily White, Maudie Scott (3, 4, 5, 6), Ms. Saunders (8).

150. The concluding photograph in this chapter is a little more up to date, taken of a mixed class at Green Lawn School, New Inn in about 1955. Most of the names are known as follows, left to right - Mr. Wilcox (teacher), Willie Herbert, ?, ?, Trevor Stokes, Christine Bigham, Hilary Robinson, Gerald Bamford, Janice Butcher, June Butt, Mr. Hayward (Head). 3rd row: Tom Jones, Paul Jarrett, Peter Jarrett, Russell Giles, Roy Donovan, Simon Jones, Paul Greenhalgh, Brian Page and David Thomas. 2nd row: ?, ?, ?, Elizabeth Roberts, Christine ?, Ms. Carroll, Ms. Adkins, Rosemary Brown, Susan Tibbs and Julie Harvey. Front: Nigel Tamplin, Michael Thomas, Tommy Tremlett, Russell Dobbs, Michael Chant, Marsden Smith, Roger Williams, Howard Rees and David Garrett.

CHAPTER 6

Sport & Leisure

151. The Pontnewynydd Blues soccer team from about 1930 and the names known are - Back: Ivor Morgan, ?, Hubert Whittington, Wilf Law, Reg Jayne, ?, Reg Cooper, ?, Mr. Green, ?. Front: Mr. Hall, ?, Vic Cooper, Arthur Jones and Harry Cooper.

152. A photograph from 1927-28 titled Pontypool United A.F.C. the name 'United' usually only recognised in the rugby circles of Pontypool. Unfortunately just one player in this soccer team has been identified and he is Baden Oliver Jennings who is stood fifth from the right, in the back row.

153. From the year 1902 is seen this cricket team belonging to Trevethin Church and their names are recorded as follows, left to right - Back: W.E.H. Watkins, G.W. Hughes, W. Evans, Rev. E. Morgan (Vicar of Trevethin), E.S. Pinn, J. Drennan and J. Poulson (Umpire). Middle: E.W. Moseley (Secretary), T.B. Pearson, A.R. Hunt (Capt.), A. Stockden (Vice Capt.) and J. McCarthy. Front: F.H. Cound and Ivor Rees.

154. To past pupils of West Mon School, the faces on this photograph, believed to have been taken at Lydney Grammar School should be all too familiar. Back row, left to right: Stan W. Beese, H. Jenkins, E.J. Milton-Smith, Fred W. Hagger, Frank Witty, John H. Moseley and W.L. Purse. Seated: Mr. Illingworth, Ken Smith and Max Horton. Front: Len Morgan.

155. From the season 1910-1911 a Pontypool rugby team is seen at an away game at Abertillery Park, the season's results being Played 45, Won 26, Drawn 9, Lost 10. In the picture, left to right are - Back Row: W. Palmer (trainer), W. Phillips, A. Russell, A.E. Hickey, G. Moxley (chairman), T. Davies, F.A. Parkhouse, T. Eckley (trainer), W. Palmer (committee). Middle: S. Smith, E. Stephens, Gus Carr, Rees Thomas (capt.), B. Pritchard, T. Carter, J. Jones, W.J. Thomas. Front: S. Prosser, M. Williams, R. Lloyd. Some more players also to be noted as having played during the season but not pictured are H. Jarmon, Rhys Harrhy, F. Andrews, D.P. Jones, J.P. Jones, L. Bradley and L.H. Evans.

156. The invincible Pontypool and Blaenavon Schoolboys and Winners of the Dewar Shield 1962-63. Record for the season - Played 22, Won 19, Drew 3, Lost 0. Points for 287, Points against 49. Back row, left to right: Mr. B.E. Jones (Coach), R. Pugh, A. Curtis, G. Williams, J. Drinkwater, K. Rowles, J. Quick, D. Ford, P. Johns, A. Taylor and Mr. D. Williams (Secretary). Middle Row: A. Preece, G. Rosser, R. Cave (captain), R. Moxham (Vice captain), B. Scrivens and M. Richards. Front Row: G. Barker, K. Leek, S. Jones and L. Powell.

157. Some West Mon Old Boys are pictured during preparation for a game of rugby against the school's First XV in the 1963-64 season. Back row, left to right: Mike Neath, Eddie Bowen, V.H. 'Ox' Wilcox, John Saunders, John Griffiths, Idris Leonard, Brian Foster, Adrian Hearne, B. Evans and David Parry-Jones. Seated: Ray Dando, Robert Irving, Dave Gillard (Captain), Geoff Elliot, Gerald Davies and unknown.

158. From days when soccer was played at West Mon School, this is the First XI from the season 1912-13 when their performance was 59 goals for and 36 against. The team consists of - Back: D.R.A. Jones, H. Day, A.L. Pritchard, S.O. Jones and C. James. Middle: W.P. Alsop (vice capt.), E.N. Nicholas (capt.), Mr. R.I. Jones (headmaster), W.H. Mayers and W.H. Price. Front: A.E. Pitt and A.E. Vaughan.

159. Members of Pontypool Golf Club are pictured during an open meeting held on 6th June 1953, the club's Jubilee Day which also coincided with the Queen's coronation week. Competitions were played throughout every day, with the presentation of prizes on the evening of the 'open' to conclude the celebrations. No doubt, one hundred years of golf here, will be commemorated in true fashion in the year 2003.

160. Pontypool Park bowling green, photographed here in the 1930s, some ten years after the present club was formed in 1926. Prior to this, the old Pontypool Bowls Club which was founded in 1902, played on grounds belonging to local businessman and Justice of the Peace, Mr. Edwin Fowler who resided at Hillgrove in Upper George Street; the Pontypool club is one of the founder members of the Welsh Bowling Association.

161. The Pontnewynydd Royal Blues A.F.C. in 1928-29, when they were invincible winners of the Usk and District League 1st Division and the Langdon Cup, proudly display their trophy and medals. The gentlemen, left to right, are - Front: R. Gittings (vice capt.), W. Stokes (capt.), H. Stokes, J. Powell (mascot). Middle: F. Gibbs (trainer), A. Bowen, W. Hall, W. Vann, F. Griffiths, F. Fifield, W. Shaw (asst. trainer). Back: A. Wakefield (gen sec.), J. Tucker (chairman), T. Wakefield, W. Davies, J. Waters, A. Brooks, S. Taylor, G. Gane, L. Shorthouse (committee), R. Barnes (finance sec.).

162. A group of Penygarn youths who enjoyed playing the game of football at their regular meeting place, in a field behind The Woodlands. The photograph was taken in the 1940s and amongst the gathering are Keith Barwood, Arthur Phillips, Terry Parker, John Williams, Reg Britton, Michael Titley, Bruce Baxter, Ken Skillern and Roy Evans.

163. Landlady Mrs. Margaret Williams with some of the regulars from the Bridgend Inn Cwmffrwdoer in 1935 outside the pub. Back row, left to right: Mr. Butcher, Ted Richards, Con Jones and Abe Gauntlet. Middle: Bill Crimmins, Bill Lewis, Gerry Lee, Jim Jones, Enoch Williams, Bill Barrell, Bill Jones and Tom Cuton. Seated: Bert Parsons, Llew Davies, Margaret Williams, Bill Doyle, Jacky Lodge and Redfus Lewis.

164. Seen outside the Masons Arms public house in Griffithstown, before its complete re-building, are members of a local rifle club. During the middle of the nineteenth century, clubs of many descriptions were being established nationwide, one of which was the *'Pontypool Rifle Club'*, inaugurated in 1859 with between thirty and forty members. In those days of a widely permitted sport, members of the club were charged a fee of one guinea (£1.05) per annum for the purchase of guns and all the necessary accessories.

165. A group of local musicians, calling themselves *'The Sunbeam Dance Orchestra'* whose leader, Charles Albert is seen standing just right of centre. The orchestra entertained mainly in the Pontypool area and as well as Charles, two of his brothers were also members of the group - Edgar, seated second from the left and Gordon seated on the far right. The family, whose ancestors were of German origin, lived at number 27 Club Row, Tranch, Pontypool.

166. A total of forty-three songsters belonging to Pontypool Choral Society are pictured here in about 1948, displaying a recently-won trophy. Undoubtedly there will be readers who will recognise a few faces in the crowd and also recall being entertained by this well-talented group of singers.

167. The Girl Guides Association, an organisation established in 1910 when groups were springing up all over the country. Above are members of Griffithstown's Company pictured in about 1922. Unfortunately only four of the young ladies' names have been traced and they are - Front Row - Phyllis Samson (2nd left), Doris Saunders and Beattie Ford (6th and 7th). One other is believed to be Winnie Irvine who is stood in the back row, extreme left.

168. Another group of Girl Guides, this time the 1st Sebastopol Company from 1930 and their names are as follows, left to right - Back: Connie Price, Lily Davies, Gertie Everson, Gwen Birch, Doris Morris and Doris Foster. Middle: Joan Sumner, Edith Bailey, Joan Berry, Maisie Price (capt.), Hilda Pearson, Nellie Davies and Ethel Forrest. Front: Evelyn Griffiths, Ivy Payne, Maisie Rowlands, Lydia Gibbons, Nellie Wilkey and Ms. Manley.

169. The district of Pontypool has a long tradition of Ladies choirs throughout the years. Above, members of Panteg Women's Institute Choir are at one of their concert venues, this one being at Monmouth on 4th December 1937. Regrettably only one of the ladies has been identified, Mrs. Catherine Bird who is stood in the front centre (mother of Mr. Jeffrey Bird who kindly loaned this photograph).

170. From the 1950s, this picture is of the acclaimed Pontypool Ladies' Choir who, amongst many other achievements, won the coveted Ladies Choir competition at the Ebbw Vale National Eisteddfod in 1958. The conductor for this important event in their history was Violet Branch-Davies and the accompanist was Doris Nash-Roberts. Some of the names amongst the group, left to right are - Row 4: Mrs. Webb (3rd), Lil Fisher (5th), Cissie Hutchings (7th), Millie Schofield (8th), Mrs. Tremlett (9th). Row 3: Mrs. Richards (6th), Ms. Turner (9th), Eunice Williams (10th), Joan Davies (18th). Row 2: Doris Nash-Roberts, Violet Branch-Davies, Mrs. Roderick, Mrs. Butt, Jessie Bailey, Ceinwen Gabe. Front: Cissie Leek, ?, May Richards/Cole, Stella Baber, Louie Turner, Nora Haycock (secretary), Eva Gauntlett.

CHAPTER 7

Industrial Life

171. The Glyn Pits in the Cwm Glyn Valley which were sunk by Capel Hanbury Leigh in 1837, began coal production in the 1840s and remained so for almost ninety years. After closure in 1932, it found use until the 1960s as a pumping station for Hafodyrynys Colliery. The taller building on the left, housed a vertical steam-winding engine which was built in 1845 by the Neath Abbey Iron Works, who also supplied the Cornish-type beam pumping engine which was housed to the right of the two shafts. Both engines, thought to be the only ones of their kind in existence, still survive at this, one of the most important sites in the history of South Wales' coal-mining technology.

172. A distant look at Tirpentwys Colliery in the year 1905, when under the ownership of the Tirpentwys Black Vein Steam Coal and Coke Company Ltd. The pit was to provide employment for almost another sixty-five years until placed on the 'jeopardy list' in May 1969, when a combination of low output and geological problems rendered its closure a foregone conclusion.

173. In May 1926 the coal owners of the country presented the miners with a daunting ultimatum of accepting wage reductions ranging from twenty to forty per cent or face a 'lock out'. The Trades Union Congress, in support of the miners, called for an all-out strike throughout the country, an event that was to be known thereafter as 'The General Strike' beginning on May 3rd; it was to be a long and bitter struggle. The coal owners, who were increasingly concerned with foreign competition, wished to annul the miners' first national wage agreement, gained after World War One which included the fixed seven-hour working shift underground. Nine days into the dispute, the miners were suddenly left feeling betrayed by the T.U.C. when they called off the strike, claiming that the government now wished to negotiate a settlement. The miners however, fought on alone for a further seven months until final defeat was brought about by near starvation and abject poverty.

174. Some of the strikers who worked at Elled Colliery, Pontnewynydd are pictured in August 1926, having dug their own private mine naming it 'The Chamber of Horrors Colliery Co. Ltd.' The men involved in the operation during these desperate times are - Liston Shorthouse, Albert Wakefield, John Tucker, Morris Green, Ron Barnes, Stan Taylor, Granville Gane, Tommy Wakefield, Horace Shorthouse and Joe Britton.

175. Two local colliers in typical working attire, are pictured in about 1910 at the rear of their home in Long Row, Upper Race. Both gentlemen were employed at Blaendare Colliery Slope and are believed to be two brothers with the surname of Pearce.

176. Moving on to May 1999, and the last two working pit ponies in Great Britain completed their final working day at Pant-y-gasseg private drift mine before retiring to a life of leisure at the R.S.P.C.A.'s centre in Milton Keynes. Both Welsh cobs, Gremlin aged twenty-five and Robbie aged seven, had worked at the seventy-year-old mine for five and four years respectively, Gremlin having previously worked at a number of pits in the south-east Wales area. Mike Desmond (front) and Steve Desmond, two of the seven miners working at the mine, were saddened by their departure and the ending of a 250-year history of ponies working underground. Robbie has since been moved on to the National Mining Museum in Yorkshire.

177. The districts of Pontymoile and Pontypool Road as they appeared from an aircraft in 1939, with some former industrial landmarks in sight. Featured on the left is the Brecknock and Abergavenny canal, and adjacent to the canal the Lower Mills Works stand prominent. Originating from the first half of the nineteenth century when built as a tinplate mill, the works had various owners throughout its life including Alfred Baldwin, who in association with Messrs. Wright, Butler and Co. of Panteg fame, converted it into the manufacturing of galvanised sheets in 1895. Further right are the Phoenix Galvanising Works, acquired by Wright and Butler from Port Talbot in the mid 1890s, where it was dismantled and re-erected on the site above. At the time when this photograph was taken, both works had closed down. Directly above the Phoenix, Pilkington Bros. Glassworks, the well-known Lancashire firm is seen, built the previous year in 1938 on the site which during World War One, was occupied by the Admiralty sidings. The plant was enlarged in 1948 when output of glass sheets doubled but closure eventually came in 1975.

178. An opportunity for readers to recall some of Pontnewynydd's past industries in this photograph from about 1910. Above the bushes in the right foreground, are the buildings belonging to the Osborne Forge where, since the sixteenth century, a works had stood, once producing the renowned 'Osmond' or 'Osborne' iron, a high quality metal used in the manufacture of wire. On a map of the district produced shortly after the date of this picture, the works were shown as producing sheet steel and during some of the Second World War years, its buildings were used for storage purposes, the mills being dismantled a few years later. In the background, the sheet and galvanising works were established on the site of some previous industries, including an iron works founded in 1837, a wire works and a company producing galvanised and corrugated iron sheets. This once-major source of employment in the district finally closed its doors in 1961.

179. A group of Panteg sheet workers employed at Number 13 mill in May 1959. Just two of the names have been tracked down unfortunately and they are Mr. Johnny Evans who is at the front and directly behind, with his hands on Mr. Evans's shoulder is Mr. Derrick Hall.

180. Here is one of the industrial locomotives used at Baldwin's Ltd. Panteg named 'Italy', a 0-4-0 saddletank engine built by Messrs. Kerr Stuart in 1918 and which was formerly in use at the Baldwin works in Port Talbot, West Glamorgan. Seen above, in the 1930s, 'Italy' was withdrawn from service in 1963 and transferred to John Cashmore's Ltd. of Newport, where it was finally scrapped in 1965.

181. Among the 'less heavy' industries of the district was the factory of H.G. Stone and Company who transferred their business from Chesham in Buckinghamshire, to Pontypool Road, New Inn in 1947. This interior view of the factory was taken in the early 1950s, when some 300 workers (mainly female) were employed there manufacturing high quality soft toys. In its heyday the factory was producing up to 12,000 toys weekly, ranging from large teddy bears and dogs to miniature pram toys, all bearing the company's trade mark 'Chiltern' which became a world - recognised name for top quality products. The girls in this photograph who are producing some of the teddy bears are, from the front - Mary Hope, Violet Skillern (nee Humphreys), Eileen Chaloner (nee Bowditch), Margaret Barker and on the right Joyce Dew. The gentleman in the background is foreman Bill Gooding.

182. Some readers may remember a popular BBC Television series in the early 1980s - 'The life and times of David Lloyd George', part of an episode being filmed at the R.O.F. works Glascoed. The episode required some scenes to be authentically set in an ammunition factory during World War One and, Glascoed was given special permission to open its doors. The star Philip Madoc was at the factory playing the part of Lloyd George and a number of R.O.F. employees, seen here in period costume, served as extras. Some of the girls have been traced as Marcia Smith, Betty Evans, Dorothy Busson, Ros Pipe, Nancy Farmer, Margaret Davies and Ruby Collier. The gentleman in the bowler hat is shop manager Ivor Dando. In real terms, Glascoed was built in 1939-40 at the outbreak of war and during the six-year duration, employed 13,000 people on a 'round the clock' shift basis.

183. The former workings of the Albion Road Colliery, Pontypool. Opened by Alfred Baldwin and Co. Ltd. this colliery (a slope), was sited on the abandoned Glyn Collieries' numbers 3 and 4 pits, around the turn of the twentieth century in the Cwm Glyn valley, just over a mile from Clarence Street station. Following the 1926 General Strike, coal production ceased and by 1932 the colliery was being operated by Crumlin Valley Collieries Ltd. as a pumping unit, until it passed to the N.C.B. in 1947 when it was known as Albion Slope pumping station.

CHAPTER 8

The Railway Scene

184. Pontypool Road locomotive sheds as seen before the advent of the First World War. The original smaller shed, dating from around the middle of the nineteenth century, was situated near Coed-y-Gric Junction, later to be gradually replaced by the above, a much larger depot, sited adjacent to the Skew Fields. Pontypool Road was soon to become a vast and important marshalling yard with more than fifty sidings and running lines within its complex. The yard dealt with large numbers of goods and freight trains daily, with coal, livestock and general freight all re-marshalled into numerous trains for their various destinations. Official closure of the sheds finally came in November 1965 with a virtual shutdown of the marshalling yards by October 1967.

185. Three of Pontypool Road's loyal railway employees are seen taking a short break during shunting duties at one of the many sidings in about 1952. In the middle is engine driver Vic Evans accompanied by Harold Davies and Tom Morgan (left to right).

186. A group of workers who, on the original photograph, are described as 'Pontypool Road Mutual Improvement Class'. The men are seen in front of a G.W.R. 'Flower Class' locomotive No.4103 'Bessborough', at the coaling stage of the engine sheds in 1913. Erected in 1897-98, the coaling stage replaced an earlier structure to allow for the loading of the largest locomotives and the use of much greater-capacity coal wagons, now that coal production in south Wales was on the increase and needed to be transported as efficiently as possible.

187. In Volume One of this series of books, the original Pontypool Road Station was featured on page 113 (picture 192), its station staff awaiting the arrival of a passenger train. The photograph now seen above, was taken a few minutes later, the train having arrived with engine No. 3382 at the head. Travellers using this station, were afforded the luxury of refreshment room facilities (normally only found on much larger main-line stations) which were added in about 1862-63 and some nine years after the station first opened.

188. From the opposite side of the road bridge, seen in the background of the previous photograph, a double-headed passenger train departs from the station on its way to Abergavenny and beyond in the year 1900. As can be seen by the length of the train, platforms at Pontypool Road were now becoming inadequate and with ever-increasing volumes of traffic, it was only a matter of time before larger and much more spacious facilities were constructed.

189. Viewed from its approach road, the new Pontypool Road Junction Station which opened in 1909, comprised a large island platform. The bay on the left, situated on the south side, was used for the Vale of Neath trains via Crumlin Viaduct, while Monmouth-bound trains, via Usk, used the northern bay. The station's booking office on the far right, out-lasted the platform buildings by more than twenty years until its eventual demolition in 1993; at this juncture, almost eighty-five years of railway nostalgia came to an end at this once important junction.

190. Pontnewynydd railway station with background scenery dominated by the sheet and galvanising works as it appeared during the 1930s. The track, an extension of the former Monmouthshire Railway Company's line from Newport to Pontypool, was extended to Blaenavon in 1854, part of which was constructed on the bed of the company's canal as far as Pontnewynydd. The station served the community for almost 110 years until its closure in April 1962 when passenger services were withdrawn.

191. Engineer Charles Liddell's Clarence Street Station pictured from the westward-bound platform almost one hundred years after its construction. Built in the 1850s when the line opened as far as Crumlin, the station's platforms were further extended in 1887. This was to cope with the huge crowds that were expected for the gigantic jubilee festivities to be held in the park on Easter Monday, the park at the time still being in the ownership of the Hanbury family. Pontypool had the distinction of being the first place in the whole of Great Britain to celebrate fifty years of Queen Victoria's reign.

192. A scene looking north on the 12th October 1957 from the passenger footbridge of Crane Street Station. Behind the telegraph pole is the approach road to the station from Crane Street itself, with the Globe Hotel in sight, one of the buildings still standing today at the upper end of the street. During 1991, almost thirty years after closure, the original 'up platform' booking office was dismantled and removed to Furnace Sidings Blaenavon for re-siting; the building is still awaiting reconstruction there, as part of the Pontypool and Blaenavon Railway Society's undertaking.

193. A large group consisting of fifty-seven railway workers who were employed at Crane Street Station and Goods Yard in 1914. The sheer number of men employed at this station alone, well illustrates the importance of the steam railway era, providing means of communication and large-scale employment throughout the country.

194. A Newport-bound passenger train headed by 5700 class 0-6-0 pannier tank No.7736, passes over Crane Street's bridge, as it approaches the station's down side platform in August 1959. This type of engine, introduced in 1929, proved very popular with footplatemen and was originally designed for light goods and shunting purposes. Newport Ebbw Junction was the allocation for engine 7736, it finally being withdrawn from service in 1962.

195. Situated just south of Coed-y-Gric Junction on the Eastern Valley line, Panteg and Griffithstown Station with its staggered platform design, is viewed looking northwards from the down side platform. This picture, taken in the year 1900 when Mr. James Frank Ernest Harris was stationmaster, has been reproduced from a surviving glass lantern slide.

196. Residents of Cwmffrwdoer have witnessed quite a few changes since this scene was pictured from the rear of Tirpentwys Terrace, probably during the 1930s. Taking place is the renewal of the upper part of the old road bridge that once spanned the railway near Branches Fork Junction, with the two steam-powered cranes in the process of placing one of the side girders into position. In the background are Chapel Road to the left, and Hanbury Road opposite, the two forming the junction with Plas-y-Coed Road, which is just out of the picture, on the right.

197. Glascoed, one of Pontypool's branch line halts situated on the Pontypool Road to Usk line, was opened on 16th May 1927. The halt, pictured here in the 1940s and positioned on the 'up line' was originally sited on the opposite side, having been moved in April 1938. A larger halt at Glascoed was built for the Royal Ordnance Factory workmen's trains and was brought into use in 1939. Other halts used by the R.O.F. workers were known as 'East Access' and 'Glascoed Crossing'.

198. Following the 1914-18 war, the government of the day elected to reduce inflated wages in order to make British goods more competitive in world markets. A 'definitive' wage offer was received by the railway workers on 19th September 1919, when it was found that from 1st January 1920, while footplate grades received an increase, with the addition of a generous war bonus, other conciliation grades would get wage reductions varying from one shilling (5p) to sixteen shillings (80p) a week. On 27th September a strike began with 57,000 members of the A.S.L.E.F. union joining N.U.R. members, making the stoppage the most complete so far seen on the railways. The government subsequently climbed down on 5th October, when plans to extend the strike to other trades were seriously discussed, with terms of the settlement to include amongst other agreements, stabilization of existing earnings. The photograph seen above is of the 'Pontypool Road Strike Committee' outside Griffithstown school.

Then and Now

199./200. Preceding the construction of Pontypool's library and its opening in 1908, the above view of Commercial Street from Hanbury Road has changed somewhat over the past ninety-five years. The development of the street progressed gradually during the following fifty years or so, but many of its premises now stand unoccupied, leaving this once busy part of the town, a desolate area for today's shopper.

201./202. More than ninety years have passed since George Street above was pictured and, as may be seen, a few alterations have taken place during this period. The most obvious being the area on the immediate left, where these days, a road passes through where the former buildings once stood. Opposite, some of the original premises still stand firm, but, a few of those nearest the camera have been replaced in more recent times.

203./204. On April 3rd 2000, the historical Pontypool and Abersychan Joint Memorial Gates at the Italian Gardens' entrance to Pontypool Park were destroyed, when the fifty-foot high tree on the left of the above picture was uprooted in high winds and sent crashing down on this elaborate structure. Unlike the ornamental side gates and railings which were patterned in 1924, the central section originated from the nineteenth century and was previously used in connection with Park House, when owned by the Hanbury family. The gates are presently in the process of being re-made as authentically as possible, using original and replacement parts.

205./206. The top photograph is of Crane Street Station in about 1915 when the railway, was for many people, the only means of communication from one town or village to another. The bottom photograph taken in the year 2000, which the younger generation will easily recognise, is viewed a short distance from the roundabout at the entrance to Pontypool's top car park.

207./208. Quite a change has taken place at Blaendare since being photographed above in the 1950s, when the valley's train service was available to local residents. The newly-built road system, the building of which disrupted the community for a few years, has now transformed the area immensely and the Cwmynyscoy Viaduct, seen in the distance, is just a memory from the past, after standing solidly for almost 150 years. Today's view below, shows how much times have changed.

209./210. The imposing former Pontypool and District Hospital, viewed at its side entrance some sixty years ago and photographed again in July 2000. Still standing vacant since its closure in the early 1990s, a group of dedicated conservationists are, at the time of printing of this book, in the process of applying for 'listed building' status. The matter is presently in the hands of The Gwent Health Authority and Torfaen Borough Council in association with CADW, who will decide the future of this stately-looking structure.

211./212. New Inn's main thoroughfare seen in about 1905 and in July 2000. Some changes and additions to the scenery include, the removal of the stone wall and gate entrance, now replaced by a roadway and pedestrian safety railings, together with some familiar double yellow lines. The buildings on the right, apart from the nearest shop premises, appear not to have altered a great deal during the ninety-five year timespan.

213./214. Two views of Windsor Road, Griffithstown at the junction with Oxford Street and Hill Street. A number of shop fronts have seen some modernisation and the corner gas lamp, together with the upper bay window of the premises on the immediate left have been removed. However, the street is still easily recognisable after a period spanning some eighty years.

215./216. A little more than forty years separate these final two photographs and the changes are quite striking. The more mature reader will probably remember the above scene from 1959, which shows the long gone railway complex at Pontypool Road engine sheds. The scenery here has changed almost beyond recognition with a major bypass now occupying part of the site.

A Message of Appreciation from the Author

I would like to extend sincere thanks to a number of friends and acquaintances listed below, whose help with the loan of some photographs and accompanying information has been invaluable in the production of this book. If by chance, I have inadvertently omitted anyone, please accept my humble apologies.

I wish to thank my wife Margaret, whose continued tolerance, understanding and opinions have played such a vital role. Also I am indebted to fellow local author Malcolm Thomas, for his usual professional guidance and advice throughout.

Mr. Roger Appleby, Mr. Louis Bannon, Mr. Jeffrey Bird, Mr. and Mrs. David Boddington, Mr. Trevor Cole, Mr. Reg Cooper, Mr. Caleb Counsell, Mr. Cliff Cox, Mrs. Beryl Davies, Mr. Gerald Davies, Mr. Roy Evans, Mrs. Diane Fehners, Mrs. Pam Fitzgerald, Hywel Gabe, Mr. and Mrs. Gordon Griffiths, Mrs. Barbara Gulliford, Mrs. Eleanor Hall, Mrs. Bessie Harding, Mr. and Mrs. J. Harding, Bev and Gill Harris, Mrs. Violet Haynes, Mr. Alan Hodge, Mr. Walford Hutchings, Mr. Bert Howells, Mrs. Doris James, Mr. and Mrs. Melvin Jennings, Peter and Therese Jones, Mrs. Loader, Mr. Eric Loader, Mrs. Christine Manley, Mr. Philip Mayers, Mrs. Margaret Pead, Mr. Ray Rappel, Mrs. Marge Roberts, Mr. John Saunders, Mrs. Violet Skillern, Mrs. Beryl Thomas, Mr. Tommy Tremlett, Mrs. Tyler, Mr. and Mrs. Glyn Watkins, Mr. Steve Warman, Mr. H. Williams, Mr. John S. Williams, Mrs. Shirley Winmill.

Below is a selection of further titles available. Please send stamp to the Publishers for a detailed list.

Pictorial Memories of Old Abersychan
by Bryan Roden & Malcolm Thomas
ISBN 1 874538 52 2
- **Volume 1**

Pictorial Memories of Old Pontypool
by Bryan Roden
ISBN 1 874538 86 7
- **Volume 1**

Blaenavon Through the Years
by Malcolm Thomas & John Lewis
ISBN 0 9512181 0 7
- **Volume 2**

Blaenavon Through the Years
by Malcolm Thomas & John Lewis
ISBN 0 9512181 3 1
- **Volume 3**

Blaenavon Through the Years
by Malcolm Thomas & John Lewis
ISBN 1 874538 10 7
- **Volume 1**

Brynmawr, Beaufort and Blaina in Photographs
by Malcolm Thomas
ISBN 1 874538 15 8
- **Volume 2**

Brynmawr, Beaufort and Blaina in Photographs
by Malcolm Thomas
ISBN 1 874538 26 3
- **Volume 1**

Remember Abergavenny
by Louis Bannon
ISBN 1 874538 75 1
- **Volume 1**

Look Back at Old Abertillery
by Malcolm Thomas & Ray Morris
ISBN 1 874538 37 9

The Aneurin Bevan Inheritance
by Gareth Jones
ISBN 1 874538 17 4

The Place-Names of Eastern Gwent
by Graham Osborne & Graham Hobbs
ISBN 1 874538 91 3

Caerleon 'Scenes Past'
by Norman Stevens
ISBN 1 874538 71 9

Glimpses of Gwent
by Gareth D. John
ISBN 1 874538 12 3

Old Abercarn Urban District
by David Taylor
ISBN 1 874538 57 3

Hills of Fire and Iron
by Peter Morgan Jones
ISBN 0 9512181 9 0

Welsh Roots & Branches
by Gareth Jones
ISBN 0 9524176 0 X
- **Volume 1**

A Look at Old Tredegar in Photographs
by Philip Prosser
ISBN 0 9512181 4 X
- **Volume 2**

A Look at Old Tredegar in Photographs
by Philip Prosser
ISBN 1 874538 81 6